To: Isabella
I love you, sweetie
From: Grandmother Gloria
"2005"

For Matthew McCarthy—D.D.M.

With love for my mom, from funny little me.—J.B.H.

© 2005 Dandi Daley Mackall.

© 2005 Standard Publishing, Cincinnati, Ohio.

A division of Standex International Corporation.

All rights reserved. Printed in China.

Project editor: Robin Stanley.

Cover and interior design: Marissa Bowers.

Scripture quotations are taken from The Holy Bible, New Living Translation, copyright © 1996.

Used by permission of Tyndale House Publishers, Inc., Wheaton, IL. 60189.

All rights reserved.

12 11 10 09 08 07 06 05   9 8 7 6 5 4 3 2 1

Library of Congress Cataloging-in-Publication Data

Mackall, Dandi Daley.

Jesus in me / written by Dandi Daley Mackall ; pictures by Jenny B. Harris.

p. cm. -- (My favorite verses)

ISBN 0-7847-1534-3 (case bound picture book)

1. Christian life--Juvenile literature. 2. Fruit of the Spirit--Juvenile literature.

I. Harris, Jenny. II. Title. III. Series: Mackall, Dandi Daley. My favorite verses.

BV4571.3.M23 2005   242'.62--dc22   2004017972

MY FAVORITE VERSES

The fruit of the Spirit is
JESUS IN ME

Written by Dandi Daley Mackall   Pictures by Jenny B Harris

STANDARD PUBLISHING
CINCINNATI, OHIO

When I get up early,
pull my crayons out,
and I'm so excited
that I want to shout,

Then I draw a picture for my mom and dad
'cause I know that getting it
will make them glad . . .

that's love.

That's Jesus in me!
The fruit of the Spirit is love.

The Holy Spirit . . . will produce this kind of fruit in us: love, joy, peace, patience, kindness, goodness, faithfulness, gentleness, and self-control.
Galatians 5:22, 23

Feeling good and cheerful on a cloudy day,
filled with giggly laughter
when I'm hard at play,
when I lose at soccer, and it's still okay . . .

That's Jesus in me!
The fruit of the Spirit is joy.

The Holy Spirit . . . will produce this kind of fruit in us:
love, joy, peace, patience, kindness, goodness, faithfulness, gentleness, and self-control.
Galatians 5:22, 23

When we're getting cranky
'cause it's late at night,
but I say, "I'm sorry,"
when we start to fight,

Then before you know it,
everything's all right . . .

that's peace.

That's Jesus in me!
The fruit of the Spirit is peace.

The Holy Spirit . . . will produce this kind of fruit in us:
love, joy, peace, patience, kindness, goodness, faithfulness, gentleness, and self-control.

Galatians 5:22, 23

When we drive to Grandma's
and it takes *so* long,
and I feel like whining, but I know it's wrong,
and from deep inside me comes a Jesus song . . .

that's patience.

That's Jesus in me!
The fruit of the Spirit is patience.

The Holy Spirit . . . will produce this kind of fruit in us: love, joy, peace, patience, kindness, goodness, faithfulness, gentleness, and self-control.
Galatians 5:22, 23

When a friend falls down,
and he scrapes his knee,

And the one who rushes there to help is me,
then I kneel and help him up so carefully . . .

that's kindness.

That's Jesus in me!
The fruit of the Spirit is kindness.

The Holy Spirit . . . will produce this kind of fruit in us:
love, joy, peace, patience, kindness, goodness, faithfulness, gentleness, and self-control.
Galatians 5:22, 23

If I help my neighbor, and I shovel snow,
but I keep it secret, only God will know.
Something good's inside me, and I let it grow . . .

that's goodness.

That's Jesus in me!
The fruit of the Spirit is goodness

The Holy Spirit . . . will produce this kind of fruit in us: love, joy, peace, patience, kindness, goodness, faithfulness, gentleness, and self-control.
Galatians 5:22, 23

When I call my grandpa,
who is very old,

Or I walk the puppy without being told,
and I don't forget it
when the weather's cold . . .

that's faithfulness.

That's Jesus in me!
The fruit of the Spirit is faithfulness.

The Holy Spirit . . . will produce this kind of fruit in us:
love, joy, peace, patience, kindness, goodness, faithfulness, gentleness, and self-control.
Galatians 5:22, 23

When I mind my manners and don't push in line,
when I hold my brother and I'm glad he's mine,
or say "please" and "thank you,"
it's a real good sign . . .

that's gentleness.

That's Jesus in me!
The fruit of the Spirit is gentleness.

The Holy Spirit . . . will produce this kind of fruit in us: love, joy, peace, patience, kindness, goodness, faithfulness, gentleness, and self-control.

Galatians 5:22, 23

When I want more candy,
but I keep my cool,

or I stop from running
at the swimming pool,

And I don't splash others
if it breaks a rule . . .

that's self-control.

That's Jesus in me!
The fruit of the Spirit is self-control.

The Holy Spirit . . . will produce this kind of fruit in us:
love, joy, peace, patience, kindness, goodness, faithfulness, gentleness, and self-control.
Galatians 5:22, 23

Bearing fruit for Jesus is no mystery.
I just act like Jesus 'cause he lives in me.
And he makes me everything that I can be—

that's all.

That's Jesus in me!
Jesus in you and me.

The Holy Spirit . . . will produce this kind of fruit in us: love, joy, peace, patience, kindness, goodness, faithfulness, gentleness, and self-control.
Galatians 5:22, 23

Galatians 5:22, 23

But when the Holy Spirit controls our lives,
he will produce this kind of fruit in us:

love,

joy,

peace,

patience,

kindness,
goodness,
faithfulness,
gentleness,
and self-control.